For Marianne & Julius

A LOEWENHERZ-CREATIVE BOOK

Published by LoewenHerz-Creative 2014

Safety Goose: Children's Safety – One Rhyme at a Time
Text Copyright © 2014 Yvonne Jones
Illustrations Copyright © 2014 Yvonne Jones

Printed in the USA.

All inquiries should be sent to
info@LoewenHerz-Creative.com

www.LoewenHerz-Creative.com

ISBN-13: 978-0-692-02397-6
ISBN-10: 0-69202-397-6

LoewenHerz-Creative Publishers

NOTE TO PARENTS:

Memorizing information such as an address and a phone number can be quite difficult for little children. Yet, knowing this information is so vital. Children love to sing, and they love their nursery rhymes. So what better way to help them remember their address than with the help of a catchy and fun rhyme, set to an already familiar tune?

This book covers everything you need to teach your child about personal safety, including stranger safety, important personal information, and what to do when lost. Every parent wants their children to be safe; and safety begins by educating them early about situations your little ones might find themselves in.

All rhymes within this book are written in such a manner that they are fully customizable with your family's individual information. Simply fill in your child's data within the provided blank spaces.

Sing and repeat these songs often. Sing them with your children while they brush their teeth, use the toilet, get dressed, get ready for preschool, kindergarten, elementary school, etc. Repetition is the key to learning.

This book contains 5 supplementary cutouts to help you and your child memorize the rhymes and to remind you to apply them often. These cutouts are meant to be attached to places such as your bathroom mirror or where they are easily seen every day.

Help your children understand why it is important to learn these things (e.g., in case they get lost, in case of an emergency, etc.). But most importantly, make it fun and have a blast, for our munchkins are little for but a very short while.

Love,
Yvonne

Table of Contents

Note to Parents
My Name & Address
My Phone Number
My Birthday
Left & Right
Before I Cross A Street
My Clean-Up
Brushing My Teeth
The Number Of All Emergencies
My Week
The 12 Months Of The Year

All 4 Seasons
Say "No" To Strangers
Fire
Tying My Shoes
Stop, Drop, Roll
My Trusted List
If There's A Bully
When Lost, Where Do I Go?
Please & Thank You
Other books by this Author
Cutouts

MY NAME & ADDRESS

To the tune of "ABC"

.... is my name.
first/last name

I'm so very glad you came!

.... is my house number.
house number

.... is where I slumber.
street name

Now I know my whole address!

I'm so happy! Yes, yes, yes!

MY PHONE NUMBER

To the tune of "Muffin Man"

Dial ___-____,
phone number

___-____.
phone number

Dial ___-____,
phone number

With the area code ___.
area code

This is how I call my ....,
mom/dad/person

Call my ...., call my ....,
mom/dad/person mom/dad/person

This is how I call my ....,
mom/dad/person

With the area code ___.
area code

MY BIRTHDAY

To the tune of "Hot Cross Buns"

I am ....
_{age}

I am ....
_{age}

.... is my birthday month.
_{birthday month}

I am ....
_{age}

LEFT & RIGHT

To the tune of "This Old Man"

Left is here, right is there.

Left and right are everywhere.

Pointer up, thumbs out.

Which one makes an "L"?

Now I know my left hand well.

BEFORE I CROSS A STREET

To the tune of "Itsy Bitsy Spider"

Before I cross a street,
I look left and right.
To see if any cars are coming
Into my sight.

Red means "STOP"
When I see a crosswalk light.
Green means "GO,"
And I walk to the other side.

MY CLEAN-UP

To the tune of "Little Miss Muffet"

Here are my toys,
Bringing me joys.
I've played with them all day long.

It's time to clean up now,
And I know just how.
While singing joyfully my clean-up song.

BRUSHING MY TEETH

To the tune of "Goosey Goosey Gander"

Standing here with toothbrush,
Putting on my toothpaste.
Brushing till teeth sparkle,
To get a mouth's fresh taste.

Brushing left and right,
Brushing up and down.
Twice a day, every day,
I brush without a frown.

THE NUMBER OF ALL EMERGENCIES

To the tune of "Three Blind Mice"

911, 911.

I'll call if someone is hurt.

I'll call if someone is hurt.

That's the number of all emergencies.

That gets here ambulance and police.

They will bring back with them help and peace.

911.

MY WEEK
To the tune of "Humpty Dumpty"

Monday, Tuesday,
That's how I start.
Wednesday, Thursday,
I know them by heart.

Followed by Friday,
Saturday, and Sunday.
Let's sing it again!
What do you say?

THE 12 MONTHS OF THE YEAR

To the tune of "Teddy Bear, Teddy Bear"

January, February,
And then March.
April and May,
June's the half-year mark.
July and August,
And then September.
October, November,
Followed by December.
12 months, 12 months,
Every year.
12 months, I know them all!
Time to cheer!

ALL 4 SEASONS

To the tune of "Farmer In The Dell"

Tulips bloom in the Spring.
Heat the Summer will bring.
Leaves in Fall, beautiful.
Carols in the Winter we'll sing.

SAY "NO" TO STRANGERS

To the tune of "London Bridge"

I never go with strangers,
Not in their house, not in their car.
I never go with strangers.
No, no, no, sir.

I never take a stranger's candy,
Not a treat, no matter how nice.
I never take a stranger's candy.
Instead, I'll tell a grown-up.

FIRE
To the tune of "Jack & Jill"

When a fire alarm rings really loud,
Calmly get outside.
Stay down below the smoke,
and never, ever hide.

Once outside, don't go back in,
No matter what's left behind.
Get help and call 911,
Always keep safety in mind.

TYING MY SHOES

To the tune of "Brother John"

Lace in left hand.
Lace in right hand.
Criss cross like an "x."
Criss cross like an "x."
One of those goes under,
All the way through.
Pull tight and see what's next.
Pull tight and see what's next.

Bunny ear in left hand.
Bunny ear in right hand.
Criss cross like an "x."
Criss cross like an "x."
One of those goes under,
All the way through.
Pull and then relax.
Pull and then relax.

STOP, DROP, ROLL

To the tune of "Row, Row, Row Your Boat"

If your clothes catch on fire,
Don't run all about.
Stop, drop, roll around,
Until all flames are out.

MY TRUSTED LIST

To the tune of "Old MacDonald"

Who are the people on my trusted list?
With whom is it safe to go?
I only go with people on my trusted list,
With whom it's safe to go!

.... here, ... there.
person 1   person 2

Here ...., there ....,
person 3   person 4

And of course ....!
person 5

These are the people on my trusted list,
With whom it's safe to go.

IF THERE'S A BULLY AND YOU SEE IT

To the tune of "If You're Happy And You Know It"

If somebody is rude and not nice, say "No, thank you!"

If somebody is rude and not nice, ask "Why are you rude?"

If somebody is rude and not nice,

Walk away and do not fight.

Instead, go and tell a grown-up to help you.

WHEN LOST, WHERE DO I GO?

To the tune of "Five Little Monkeys"

Not all strangers are dangerous and bad;
But looks alone won't tell me that.
Therefore, when lost and I don't know where to go,
I find another Mommy with children in tow.

I tell her I am lost and I need help;
That I can't find my .... by myself.
mom/dad/etc.
Mommies are helpful and that's where I'll be safe;
They'll know what to do and how to behave.

PLEASE AND THANK YOU
To the tune of "Hey Diddle Diddle"

Say please and thank you,

Welcome and bless you.

Be friendly in every way.

For what you give to others, you will receive,

Each and every day.

Being a military spouse, *Yvonne Jones* and her military family are constantly changing their place of residence and phone numbers. In an attempt to help her little one retain this ever changing but vital information, she decided to find an easier and fun way that combines her son's love of singing with the necessity of recalling his address.

She currently lives here, but tomorrow, she'll be living someplace else...

OTHER WORKS BY THIS AUTHOR

Got Garbage – The Garbage Book For The Biggest Garbage Fan

Teeny Totty™ Uses Mama's Big Potty – Transition From Potty Chair To Toilet

Closing The Gap – Understanding Your Service(wo)man

Thank You

Thank you for reading *SAFETY GOOSE*. If you and your little one(s) enjoyed this book, please be so kind and leave a review on Amazon. As an author, there is nothing more fulfilling and rewarding than hearing from readers.

BRUSHING MY TEETH

To the tune of "Goosey Goosey Gander"

Standing here with toothbrush,
Putting on my toothpaste.
Brushing till teeth sparkle,
To get a mouth's fresh taste.

Brushing left and right,
Brushing up and down.
Twice a day, every day,
I brush without a frown.

Placement idea: bathroom mirror, etc.

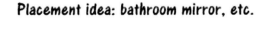

MY NAME & ADDRESS
To the tune of "ABC"

.... is my name.
first/last name

I'm so very glad you came!

.... is my house number.
house number

.... is where I slumber.
street name

Now I know my whole address!

I'm so happy! Yes, yes, yes!

Placement idea: fridge, general kitchen area, etc.

MY PHONE NUMBER

To the tune of "Muffin Man"

Dial ___ - _____,
phone number
___ - ___.
phone number
Dial ___ - _____,
phone number
With the area code ___.
area code

This is how I call my ....,
mom/dad/person
Call my ...., call my ....,
mom/dad/person   mom/dad/person
This is how I call my ....,
mom/dad/person
With the area code ___.
area code

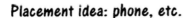

Placement idea: phone, etc.

THE NUMBER OF ALL EMERGENCIES

To the tune of "Three Blind Mice"

911, 911.
I'll call if someone is hurt.
I'll call if someone is hurt.
That's the number of all emergencies.
That gets here ambulance and police.
They will bring back with them help and peace.
911.

Placement idea: phone, etc.

TYING MY SHOES

To the tune of "Brother John"

Lace in left hand.
Lace in right hand.
Criss cross like an "x."
Criss cross like an "x."
One of those goes under,
All the way through.
Pull tight and see what's next.
Pull tight and see what's next.

Bunny ear in left hand.
Bunny ear in right hand.
Criss cross like an "x."
Criss cross like an "x."
One of those goes under,
All the way through.
Pull and then relax.
Pull and then relax.

Placement idea: near the front door, etc.

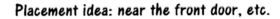